Brownie Quest

Follow the Trails . . . of the
ELF Adventure and the Three Keys

Girl Scouts of the USA

CHAIR, NATIONAL BOARD OF DIRECTORS	CHIEF EXECUTIVE OFFICER	EXECUTIVE VICE PRESIDENT, MISSION TO MARKET	VICE PRESIDENT, PROGRAM DEVELOPMENT
Connie L. Lindsey	**Anna Maria Chávez**	**Jan Verhage**	**Eileen Doyle**

SENIOR DIRECTOR, PROGRAM RESOURCES: **Suzanne Harper**

ART DIRECTOR: **Douglas Bantz**

WRITERS: **Ann Redpath, Laura Tuchman**

CONTRIBUTORS: **FableVision, Tia Disick**

ILLUSTRATOR: **Helena Garcia**

DESIGNER: **Parham Santana**

First published in 2008 by Girl Scouts of the USA
420 Fifth Avenue, New York, NY 10018
www.girlscouts.org

ISBN: 978-0-88441-711-8

Printed in Italy

4 5 6 7 8 9/16 15 14 13 12

Photo of Wangari Maathai, page 43, by Martin Rowe, Yale Club, New York City, 2002.
Haiku activity on page 29 adapted from *Haiku: Asian Arts and Crafts for Creative Kids* by
Patricia Donegan, Tuttle Publishing, a member of the Periplus Publishing Group.
Recipes on pages 56–57 adapted from these GSUSA publications: *Brownie Girl Scouts Sports
Diary, Brownie Try-It Book,* and *Junior Girl Scouts Sports Diary.*
Portrait on page 72: National Portrait Gallery, Smithsonian Institution/Art Resource, NY

The women mentioned in this book are examples of how women have used their voice in the world.
This doesn't mean that GSUSA (or you) will agree with everything they have ever done or said.

MIX
Paper from
responsible sources
FSC® C018290
www.fsc.org

Text printed on Fedrigoni Cento 40 percent de-inked,
post-consumer fibers and 60 percent secondary recycled fibers.
Covers printed on Prisma artboard FSC Certified mixed sources.

Contents

Benvenuti

Willkommen

HUAN YING

Swaagatam

WELCOME
TO THE BROWNIE QUEST

Ant chukoa

You are about to:
Meet new friends.
Uncover the secret of ELF.
Search for three keys.
Find out what they open!

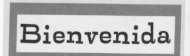
Bienvenida

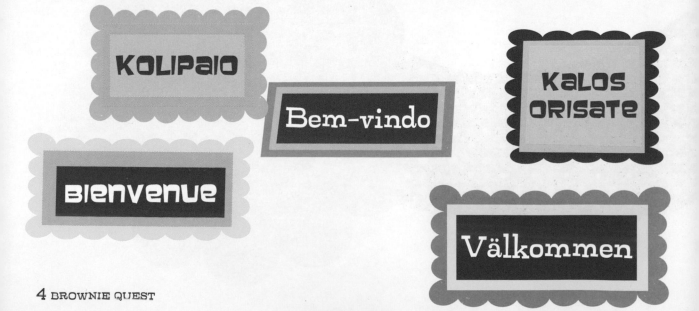

Kolipaio

Bem-vindo

Kalos Orisate

Bienvenue

Välkommen

On this quest,

you have two trails to try.

Visit the **Trail of the ELF Adventure** anytime you like. There you'll meet Brownie friends Campbell, Jamila, and Alejandra — and a very special elf who likes to ELF around. Soon you'll know what ELF *really* means.

When you get together with Brownie friends in your community, you'll explore the **Trail of the Three Keys**. Go ahead, take a peek. Curious to uncover the mystery behind all the blank spaces? Good! Curiosity is the best thing to take with you on a quest!

A quest is about looking for something important. What will you find?

PART 1
Trail
of the
ELF
Adventure

This trail has a clubhouse.
Come on in and meet some new Brownie friends!

Campbell lives with her mom and her little sister, Sage — and her new dog, Tango. She is happiest outdoors, especially on her skateboard. Social studies and Spanish are her favorite subjects. She has just moved to Green Falls, and her family is still trying to unpack. In the summer, she likes to grow tomatoes with her mother in their garden.

Jamila has lived in Green Falls her whole life. She lives with her dad and her brother, TJ. They have a cat named Fredrick. Jamila loves to read and she likes to take things apart just to see how they work. Sometimes she has trouble putting them back together. Her dad wasn't too happy when she opened up the family computer.

Alejandra lives just outside Green Falls — on a big *rancho* with her parents and her *abuela* and *abuelo*. Alejandra loves animals, especially horses. She has a pony named Ladybug. She spends a lot of time going on hikes with her *abuelo*. He has taught her a lot about the outdoors. Alejandra also loves to paint and draw, especially pictures of the woods around the *rancho*.

Brownie Elf loves being a Brownie. She has a Scottish grandmother who knows everything about Brownies. "Don't be afraid to mix old treasures with new adventures," Grandmother Elf says. She also tells Brownie Elf that in order to be a full elf, she needs to help a group of Girl Scout Brownies. And so she sends young Brownie Elf on a quest to find those Girl Scouts.

Brownie Stories

In Girl Scouts, Brownies have always been linked to elves who do good deeds.

Even before there were Girl Scouts, there were Brownies — and lots of stories about them. Back then, Brownies *were* elves: tiny creatures who did helpful work.

In Girl Scout Brownie stories, there is always one elf with one very big job: making girls see that they are capable of remarkable things, especially if they team up.

It's fun to tell stories about Girl Scout Brownies and their adventures with an elf. This quest has a Brownie story specially made for you.

You've already met the three main characters — Campbell, Jamila, and Alejandra. They are all 9 years old.

The three girls discover that they all have bracelets that look exactly alike — almost! Each bracelet has a different letter on its charm, and all the letters seem to go together. It makes perfect sense for the three girls to join together. As they do, an elf appears and invites the girls on their first adventure.

To learn what happens, turn the page. As you read about the girls and their meeting place, you may find yourself wanting to form your very own Brownie ELF Team.

You're in for quite an adventure!

Here's a clue Grandmother Elf gives Brownie Elf:

Explore, Link Arms, and Fly into Action

What do those big letters spell?

Want to know more? Read on!

BROWNIES AROUND THE WORLD

Campbell, Jamila, and Alejandra — and you — have Brownie friends all around the world. Do you know what a Brownie is called in other countries? See if you can figure out the names. **Match the names below with their country.**

Pouli   Sweden

Bluebird   Yemen Republic

Hadita   Thailand

Lechwe Guide   Italy

Beaver Guide   Greece

Lupetta (Wolf Cub)   Mexico

Zahrat   Zambia

The ELF Adventure:
Explore, Link Arms, and Fly

Chapter 1
Campbell's New Friends

It was Campbell's first day at her new school. She woke up feeling lonely and missing Cora and Chandra, her **absolute**

best friends in the entire world. And, oh, how she missed their flower garden and all the time they spent together there! She felt a little better when she met her new teacher, who had the biggest smile ever. And at lunchtime, two girls, Jamila and Alejandra, asked Campbell to eat lunch with them.

As Campbell bit into her peanut butter sandwich, she suddenly said to Alejandra, "Mffh aav dat beckse, doo!" The girls giggled, and Campbell tried again after she had swallowed. "I have that bracelet, too!" Campbell pulled on her sleeve and straightened out the bracelet. "It was my grandmother's."

> Words Worth Knowing!
> **Absolute** means perfect, pure, and complete. When something is absolute, you can be completely sure about it.

Words Worth Knowing!
Amazement means being very surprised. Sometimes your eyes even open wide. When you look at something in amazement, you can be sure it is truly special!

Jamila and Alejandra looked at each other in **amazement**. "I have that bracelet, too!" said Jamila, and she pulled up the sleeve of her sweater to show her bracelet. "Mine was my mother's. Ali's was her mother's, too!"

The girls huddled over their bracelets. They were exactly the same except for one thing: the charms that dangled from them. One had an E on it, one had an L, and one had an F.

"I wonder why they're different?" said Alejandra.

"Maybe they're supposed to spell something," said Jamila, "like *lef*."

"Or *fel*," offered Campbell.

"Um, call me crazy," said Alejandra, "but how about *elf*?"

The girls laughed. Campbell smiled. "You're smart, Ali! We should all play after school! Can you?"

"Yeah, that would be great!"

Campbell took a sip of her juice. "I heard they're planning to build a snack shop near the new playground in the park! That will be so cool."

"Yes," said Alejandra sadly. "We heard."

Jamila patted Alejandra on the back. "Ali is sad because of our tree family."

"Tree family?" asked Campbell.

"Well, it's not really *our* family, or even a *family*. We just call it that. There's a really, really old tree with three other trees around it — like a family. Two trees are **regular**, and there's one new little tree — all in a group. But the old tree and one of the other trees will come down before they build the shop."

Words Worth Knowing!
Regular means normal or seen or used every day. If something is regular, it is not special. But a regular tree is still something special, just because it's a tree!

"No way," said Campbell. "Don't they know we should be saving trees?"

Alejandra **shrugged**. "I don't know, and I'm not sure how to tell them!"

"Well, we definitely have to tell them!" cried Jamila.

Suddenly the lunch bell rang. "We've got to figure this out," said Campbell. "Let's meet after school in the park!"

After school, the three girls met at Green Falls Park. They sat in the grass near the tree family.

"So, what's our plan?" asked Campbell.

"Well, we have to let anyone and everyone know about the tree family — and why they need trees. We all need trees. We can't have a world without trees!" Alejandra brushed the hair from her eyes, frustrated.

"Why do we need trees again?" Jamila asked quietly. Then she remembered Ali's *rancho* and its beautiful woods — and how fresh the air smelled. She put her chin in her hand, and her bracelet jingled out from the sleeve of her sweater and looked all shiny in the sun.

"Jamila, the charm on your bracelet has words on the edge of it!" exclaimed Campbell. "Ali, does yours?"

The girls took off their bracelets and placed them side by side in the grass.

"Hmmm . . . so if we put our charms together to spell E-L-F, then look! These words around the edge match up, too!" said Jamila.

"Look at the funny shape our charms all make," Campbell joined in.

"Almost like a key!" Alejandra shouted.

The girls began to read the words that started on the edge of the first charm and finished on the edge of the third.

"Twist me . . . and turn me . . . and show me the . . . elf. I looked in the water and saw _____."

Suddenly the charms began to **glow**. The girls jumped up and stepped back. The bracelets gave off a yellowish light that glowed all around the trees and up toward the sky.

Before the girls could say another word, a small elf stood in front of them!

Words Worth Knowing!
Glow means to shine with a bright and warm light. Charms can glow. The moon glows, and lightbulbs glow. Happy people also glow!

FRIENDSHIP GAME

"Mffh aav dat beckse, doo!" How does Campbell's peanut butter sandwich sentence translate into "new friend" talk?

In the story, Campbell's words mean

In your life, what are some good ways for starting to make a friend?

Have you ever tried playing a question game for getting to know someone? Ask some silly questions and some not-so-silly ones — like:

- If you were an animal, what would you be?

- What do you like to eat best?

- What's a joke you love to tell?

- What's the funniest/weirdest thing you and your family like to do?

Or do some silly things. With your Girl Scout friends, try some of these:

- Line up by birthdays.

- Line up by the colors of your socks.

- Line up alphabetically.

Then turn and put your hands on the shoulders of the person in back of you and wiggle and walk through the room like different animals. Try to stay connected!

What are some good ways to keep a friendship going?

Twist Me and Turn Me

> "Twist me and turn me and show me the elf.
> I looked in the water and saw_____."

Those words with the fill-in-the-blank at the end were written into the earliest Girl Scout Brownie story — and every Brownie story since.

Even Brownies who are now all grown up remember those beloved story lines and can recite them by heart — along with the missing word! You are on a new Brownie Quest with a new Brownie story, so here's a special version of the elf rhyme just for you:

Twist me and turn me and show me the elf.
I looked in the water and saw_____.
Looked in the pool but no elf did I see.
Gazing from the water I saw just me!
What rhymes with elf?
Helf, jelf, or melf?
I never heard any such word.
What rhymes with elf?
It couldn't be felf.
It could be myself.
Yes, it must be myself.
Twist me and turn me and show me the elf.
Gazing from the water
I saw myself!

Chapter 2
An Awesome Tree House

"Wow," said the elf. "You girls can read some teeny writing!"

Campbell, Jamila, and Alejandra were too surprised to speak. The elf picked up the girls' bracelets and took a closer look. "Oh, yes, these are the older models. They must have belonged to your mothers?"

Jamila and Alejandra nodded. Campbell's voice squeaked, "My grandmother."

The elf smiled. "How special!" Then she put the bracelets back down. "Well, girls, it looks like you are headed on a wonderful adventure. Remember," she said as she raised her hands up high, "you can reach the sky when you explore, link arms, and fly!" And in a blink, the elf was gone.

The girls stared at the spot where the elf had been, their mouths hanging open.

Jamila finally spoke: "What just happened?"

Campbell couldn't help laughing. "Unless we're all just crazy, an elf came to tell us that we are going on an adventure, and . . . what did she say?"

Still stunned, Alejandra spoke: "You can reach the sky when you explore, link arms, and fly."

"C'mon," said Jamilla. "We need to figure this out. Follow me!"

Jamila started running toward her backyard and her brother's abandoned tree house.

Jamila and Alejandra **scrambled** up the ladder to TJ's old tree house. Campbell followed the two other girls, feeling puzzled as she climbed.

Words Worth Knowing!
Campbell, Jamila, and Alejandra scrambled up the ladder. That means they moved fast and used their hands and their feet. But scrambled is not just a verb that means moving fast. Scrambled can also be a very scrumptious word. Especially if you like scrambled eggs! Scrambled eggs are all mixed up. So scrambled can mean all jumbled up, like a puzzle or some eggs.

"For an old tree house, this sure feels pretty solid," Campbell said, wondering whether she had said that out loud or not.

Clearing away the cobwebs around the door, Jamila reached a hand down to help Alejandra and Campbell into the tree house. Inside, it was dry and warm. Just the right amount of light came through the slats of wood, and shadows danced on the walls.

"This is *sooo* cool!" said Campbell.

"It's our **headquarters**!" said Jamila. "It used to be TJ's, but he's too old for a tree house now. We can meet here — and plan how to save the trees!"

"Yeah, trees like this one," piped up Alejandra.

"Look how big the branches are! I feel like I can see forever up here. Maybe we can even figure out why a magical elf just visited us." She rolled her eyes.

The girls burst into giggles. "So what's the name of our club?" Campbell asked.

"Name?" said Jamila.

"Yeah, we can't have a headquarters unless we first have a name!" Alejandra jumped around the tree house. "This place is awesome!"

As Alejandra jumped, her bracelet caught Campbell's eye. "The ELF House! Like our bracelets!"

"That's perfect," said Jamila. "And our next meeting will be tomorrow, right after school."

The girls climbed down from the tree house, waved to each other, and then ran home before the sun slipped below the horizon.

Chapter 3
Read a Rhyme, See an Elf

Again, Campbell was the last to climb the ladder. At the top, two big smiles on two excited faces were waiting for her.

"Great! You're here," said Alejandra. "It's time to save the tree family! It's time to call the ELF House to order!"

Campbell sat down, completing the circle of three girls. "I just checked on the way here. No one has touched the trees," she said.

"Did you see the truck?" asked Alejandra.

"No! What truck?"

"I don't know, but there were workmen in it, and they were pointing and measuring and driving on the grass."

The girls were quiet for a moment.

"OK," said Campbell, "how do we call the house to order?"

"Hmmm," thought Jamila. "Maybe we could read the rhyme again . . . the one on our bracelets?"

The girls spoke together: "Twist me and turn me and show me the elf. I looked in the water and saw myself."

The charms began to glow, and the yellow light reflected off the walls. Then the elf appeared, blinking hard.

"Look what you girls have found!" she said, turning around and looking at the tree house. The girls were as stunned as they were the first time the elf had appeared.

Campbell finally spoke: "So you show up when we read the rhyme!"

"Yup, that tends to do the trick," the elf said.

"We need some help," said Alejandra. "We're trying to save some . . ."

WE NEED HELP!

The elf interrupted Alejandra. "Yes, I know," she said, "and soon you will see that one is not as powerful as three." And with that, the elf was gone.

"What?" said Jamila. "What does that even *mean*?"

"I think it means that we have to work together," said Alejandra.

WHAT DOES THAT MEAN?

"But we *are* working together," exclaimed Jamila.

"Yes, but I think the elf means something more," Alejandra said.

"Maybe when we come together," said Campbell, "we each bring something different and special!"

"Exactly," said Alejandra.

"She's right," agreed Jamila. "Ali, you love to draw, right? And I love to fix things and build things! And Campbell . . ."

"I like talking," Campbell added. "I can talk to anyone. I can talk to a brick wall!"

The girls laughed, rolling around on the tree house floor.

"This is why we're the **ELF Team! ELF! ELF!**" the girls began to chant.

Jamila jumped up. "C'mon, let's make this place into a real headquarters!"

The girls ran around the neighborhood, collecting wood crates, an old rug, pieces of cloth — anything they could find to use in their tree house. Bringing it all back to a spot under the ladder, the girls sprang into action. Campbell swept the floor and started to wipe down the ledges, which were covered with dirt. Alejandra took all the pieces of cloth and started to string them up on the walls. Jamila took apart the wood crates and built small chairs for each of them.

By the end of the afternoon, the girls, working with the power of three, had turned their headquarters into a home.

WHAT THE BROWNIE FRIENDS CARE ABOUT

What's going on in the story "The ELF Adventure"?

What caught Jamila, Alejandra, and Campbell's attention?

Why did they care about what was happening?

Does their problem give you any ideas? Jot them down here.

Mixing Old Treasures with New Adventures

Back in the early days of Girl Scouting, Brownies were asked to do this:

Notice some living thing that interests you and "claim" it for your own.

When Jamila heard about this, she got interested in the bird called the swallow. She liked the name and the shape of the little bird with pointed wings.

Jamila's mom told her that the swallow is part of a family of birds with the Latin name Hirundinidae. When Jamila heard Hirundinidae, she got even more interested in swallows. The name sounds like "hear run dini day," so Jamila started to make up silly rhymes like:

Hear run dini day —
What's that sound you say?
Fly away on a December day.
Come back when you may.
Hear run dini day.

Do you want to try making up a silly rhyme with "hear run dini day"?

Or make up some rhymes with a silly-sounding word of your own.

FUN WITH HAIKU

the snail
slowly, slowly
climbs Mount Fuji

— Issa, 1789

Have you heard of **haiku**? Haiku is the shortest poetry in the world. It's also very popular. Why do people like it? It's part of everyday life. Haiku is all about seeing things in the world right around us. Haiku is a little like a sign that says: "Notice this!" That's all. And then the poem is over.

a frog floating
in the water jar
rain of summer

— Shiki, 1882

One more thing — Haiku is very old. It's been around for hundreds of years. Here's one about looking at a tree on a sunny, breezy morning.

morning sun and wind
lacy treetops choose
who wins

— Seka, 2008

NOW, WRITE a HaIKU OF YOUR OWN

Most often, a haiku is about outdoor life. So maybe start with a tree. (That would make Alejandra happy, right?) Think about a tree you like — or go outside and take a good look at it. Then, here's what you need to do to make a haiku:

- **Use three lines. Some people write the three lines in a short-longer-short pattern. So you might want to try that.**

- **Describe what you see with words that really paint a picture. If you are writing about a flower, don't just write "flower." Instead, for example, write "a tangerine tulip."**

- **And a haiku has a little surprise in it. So include a surprise.**

Some guide words might help you:

....
(when)

....
(where)

....
(what)

Now mix up the order. See how that works, too.

....

....

....

Haiku is a little reminder: **LIFE IS FULL OF SWEET THINGS.**

To make your haiku really special, add a drawing.

Chapter 4
How to Save the Tree Family

Sitting in their spiffy new headquarters, the girls try to decide what to do to save the trees. Finally, they decide on an "action plan":

1. Alejandra, who likes to draw, will make posters that show how trees, especially their roots, need lots of space to grow.

2. Jamila will make a chart of the trees' height and root space. Her brother, TJ, will help create the chart. Jamila will also measure the distance the new snack shop has to be from the trees to keep them safe.

3. Alejandra and Jamila will ask for a community meeting, and Campbell will talk at the meeting. She'll explain how the tree family needs to be saved and how much room the trees need. She'll use Jamila's charts to explain all this.

4. Campbell will also ask her mother to call her Uncle Roger because he works at the Park Board. She wants to talk with him before the community meeting to get some tips about how to speak to the crowd.

Together, the girls start moving forward — ready to **fly into action!**

IT'S YOUR TURN!

As the girls get ready for their big meeting, is there anything else they should do? Did the girls forget anything important in their action plan?

Write down anything they forgot:

1.

2.

3.

If you were planning the meeting, who would you invite?

What would you do at the meeting?

What might you need help with?

SKILLS TO SHARE

Brownie Elf had a suggestion for Campbell, Alejandra, and Jamila. They should use the special skills each girl has to plan how to fix their problem.

Who was good at art?

Who could talk to a brick?

Who was good at measuring things?

How did they use those skills?

LET'S DO AS BROWNIE ELF SAYS:

Think about yourself —
What are you good at?
Take an inventory.

Cooking?

CRAFTS?

COMPUTER?

What's
an inventory?
Brownie Elf says:
**"It's a list of all
the things that
you can do or that
you have."**

Good listener?

Good with little kids?

DANCE?

Jot down those special YOU skills here:

What would you like to learn?

What skills of yours do you want to share with the community?

Chapter 5
Getting Ready for the Big Meeting

The girls put up the posters all over the town. Then they focus on Jamila's main task. She needs to figure out how far from the tree family the snack shop needs to be. They measure and make notes. TJ helps sketch out a chart. Then Alejandra helps Jamila make the chart easy to read and colorful.

Campbell asks lots of kids and adults to come to the meeting to help her make her case.

The meeting is set for the next evening. The girls are nervous but excited. The meeting starts right on time, and Campbell gives her speech.

Then the girls watch as a vote is taken. The people have decided: The shop must be moved away from the trees. **The girls' plan is a success!**

IT'S YOUR TURN!

How will the adventure end?

Suppose a big thunderstorm starts rumbling right before the meeting, with strong winds that rip big branches off the oldest tree and pull the little tree up out of the ground. What would the girls do then?

Can you help them out?

Make up your own what-if. What if Campbell, Jamila, and Alejandra

Chapter 6
Reaching for the Sky

The next day the girls head to their tree house headquarters to celebrate their success. They dance and chant: "You *can* reach the sky when you explore, link arms, and fly!" They put their bracelets together and chant the refrain again and again.

Suddenly, the elf appears.

Brownie Elf is so proud of the girls. She explains to Jamila, Alejandra, and Campbell that they are now full-fledged Girl Scout Brownie leaders. And she is now a full Brownie Elf, because she has helped a group of Girl Scout Brownies! She tells the girls to look on the tree house wall under a piece of cloth that Alejandra hung.

The three girls see the directions for the Girl Scout handshake magically appear before them on the wall. They realize that they are walking in the footsteps of the many Girl Scout Brownie leaders who came before them.

What could be better than that?

Celebrate with a Ballad

Here's a Brownie Ballad to celebrate
Campbell, Jamila, and Alejandra's success! Think
up some more stanzas based on the good things
you and your Brownie friends do.

Once there were three special girls.
A silver bracelet linked them true.
When they met, each wore a charm.
E - L - F — that surely was the clue!

To what, they wondered, did it lead,
This bracelet that spelled ELF?
Talking of what mattered most
They talked about themselves.

In all the talking, they learned a lot,
And soon discovered something big:
Together they could do so much
And with no costume and no wig.

Give a hand to a mom at the park
Give your turn to someone shy
Take a stand when you'd rather run —
Link arms and you can fly.

The three were having so much fun
Exploring all there was to see.
They made themselves a Brownie Elf House,
Yet knew they missed the key.

What could it mean — this E-L-F?
Were there elves somewhere to find?
Yes! That's it! That's the key!
It's a message meant to mind!

Be like elves and do special things,
And be sure to do them well.
And if you do, the world will know,
You've made a difference all will tell.

Give a hand to a mom at the park
Give your turn to someone shy
Take a stand when you'd rather run —
Link arms and you can fly.

Big Ideas from the Brownie ELF Team

What ideas have you gotten from reading about the Brownie ELF Team? Start an Idea Bank of action projects you might like to do with Brownie friends. Put a star next to your favorite ideas. And check out some of these stories about what other Girl Scouts do!

Girls Make the World a Better Place

Girls and women have always taken action all around the world.

Every day we learn something new from our sisters.

Katie Saves Some Classes

When she was just 8 years old, Katie, a Girl Scout, formed a student-parent support group called Every Child, One Voice. Katie wanted to keep some classes that were going to be cut at her school. She thought the classes were important for everybody. Because she wanted to change the minds of the people who made the decisions, Katie got in touch with three county commissioners and one state representative. She wrote a letter to the head of the school board and even answered questions from the local media. Many people supported Katie's cause. In fact, so many people supported her that the school board decided not to cut the classes. Now a representative from Katie's Every Child, One Voice group attends all school board and PTA meetings.

"I was able to keep my teachers and classes," Katie says. "I learned through all this that my own small voice can be heard!"

This reminds me that I

A Letter from Genevieve

I had the opportunity to work with a refugee family from the Bantu tribe of Somalia. When we first met them, they had nothing but the clothes on their backs. Still, they were loving and eager to learn.

We helped the children with their schoolwork, and we took the family around so they could run errands. We would often sit with them and hear about their exile from Somalia to a refugee camp in Kenya.

We played lots of soccer because they loved the sport and it was a way we could connect without saying anything. Since soccer is a popular sport throughout the whole world, kids from different ethnic groups joined us. We had parties and a picnic to celebrate World Refugee Day. We met other refugees from all over the world who lived in Boise.

My troop worked with the refugees for a couple of months, but I continued on for a year and a half. I wonder who learned more — the refugees or me? They taught me to slow down and enjoy what life has to give me. They taught me to play hard and laugh harder. I hope that someday I can travel overseas and experience their cultures in their homelands.

Genevieve
Girl Scout Senior
Boise, Idaho

One Warm Coat

When one woman in San Francisco had a coat to give away, she wanted to make sure that a needy person did not have to pay for it. Her name is Lois Pavlow, and she started an organization called One Warm Coat.

A worker at a homeless shelter said, "One of our best memories was of the day we were running out of coats. Just then we saw the Girl Scouts of San Francisco Bay Area pull up to the door of the shelter. They filled our coatracks so that people could survive many bitterly cold nights."

It's good to remember all the everyday things I have, like

....

....

....

....

....

....

From New England to Nigeria

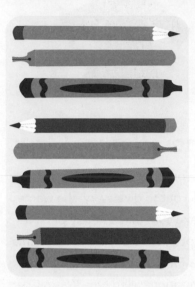

In New England, many Girl Scouts helped Teachers without Borders, an organization that provides supplies to teachers who are in places with few or no resources. These girls sent school supplies to a refugee camp in Calabar, Nigeria, and contributed materials for a new school that was being built. Some of the Girl Scouts even talked to the Nigerian girls on the phone.

The Nigerian National Youth Service Corps is using the supplies the Girl Scouts sent to get the schoolrooms ready. Girls in the United States are not trying to help "foreigners." Instead, they are learning "from and with" distant friends.

Besides notebooks and pencils, some of the items the Girl Scouts gathered to send to Nigeria were sneakers, first-aid kits, compasses, and calculators. Girl Scouts as young as Daisies helped with this project.

Pinwheels for Peace

Pinwheels for Peace was started by two art teachers in Coconut Creek, Florida. The program gives students a way to express their feelings about what is going on in the world and in their lives. On the International Day of Peace, celebrated on September 21, people all over the world express their desire for peace by "planting" pinwheels outside public places such as libraries, schools, and museums. More than 500,000 pinwheels have been planted in more than 1,350 locations around the world.

This shows that people care about peace because

....

....

....

....

....

....

Planting 20 Million Trees

Brownie friend Alejandra, who loves trees, would be pleased to know about Wangari Maathai.

🌳

Wangari was a woman from Nyeri, Kenya, in Africa. She received the highest honor in the world. That honor was the Nobel Peace Prize. Wangari won it in 2004. Why did she receive such a high honor?

🌳

Wangari studied a lot and earned a high degree to become a professor. But the most important thing Wangari did for peace was plant trees. Wangari told the people in her city in Kenya that women should plant trees to help the environment. This would make the quality of everyone's life better, she said.

🌳

Wangari helped many women plant more than 20 million trees on their farms and on lands around schools and churches. Her work is now called the Green Belt Movement.

🌳

You and 800,000
Girl Scout Brownies around the world
are on a starting line together.
You are setting off on a quest to find
three important keys.

That's big!

Along this Quest, you'll find loads of fun!
You'll make new friends, maybe read a pun.
You'll Discover things, too — talents galore.
Plus, you'll feel confident as you explore
all that you can give to this great big Quest,
including leading your family to be its best!
Then you'll Connect with sister Brownies
and Take Action to wipe out some frownies!

Plus, you'll feel so smart — yes, indeed! —
when you figure out
those three special keys!

And when we Fly into Action, look what happens!

3RD KEY STEP 3

_____

3RD KEY STEP 2

_____

3RD KEY STEP 1

Nursery School

Library

FOUND IT! 2ND KEY

_____

I ACCEPT THE BROWNIE QUEST!

Maybe the three keys mean _____, _____, and _____
While I'm searching for the keys, I hope I'll _____

_____ _____
Signed   Date

This is me!

1ST KEY STEP 1

_____

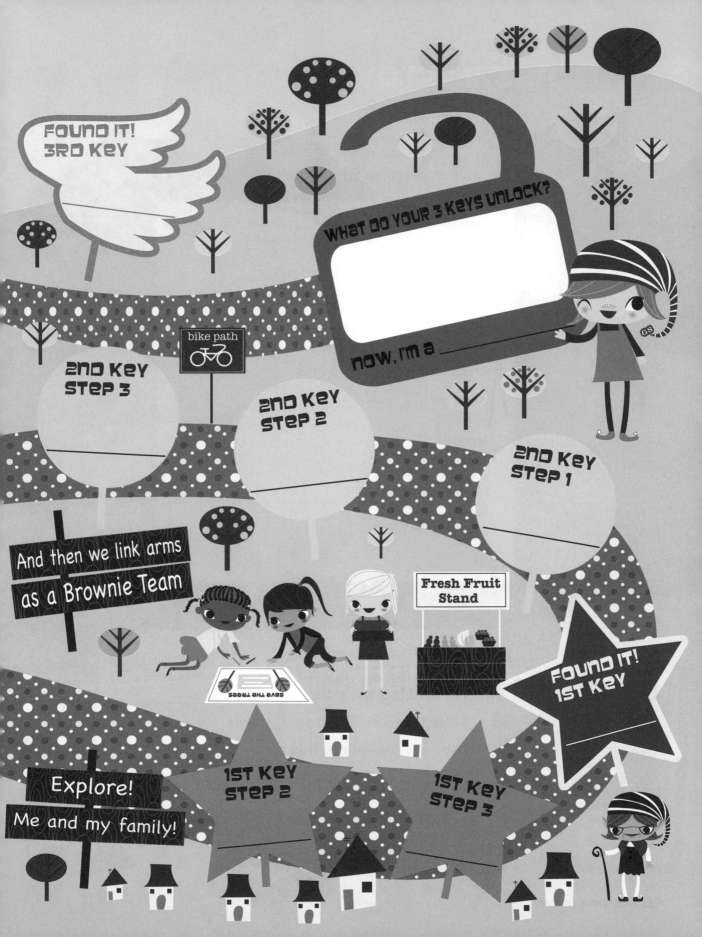

PUZZLING OVER
KEYS

Directions: See how many words you can pair up to make a combined word. One is given for you.

key .... *zookeeper*
keeper ....
zoo ....
Florida ....
chain ....
West ....
locked ....
board ....
stone ....
smith ....
lock ....
out ....
in ....

A **KEY** can also solve a problem or puzzle.

SOLVE THIS MYSTERY
Find the rhyming word from the list below to fill in the blank. Solve the mystery!

I know it's here. It's got to _____
I'm looking here and there, you _____
I must find it. The team needs _____
I see it now — it's this new _____.

we   be   see   free   key   tree   me   tea

Finding the First Key

DISCOVERING ME

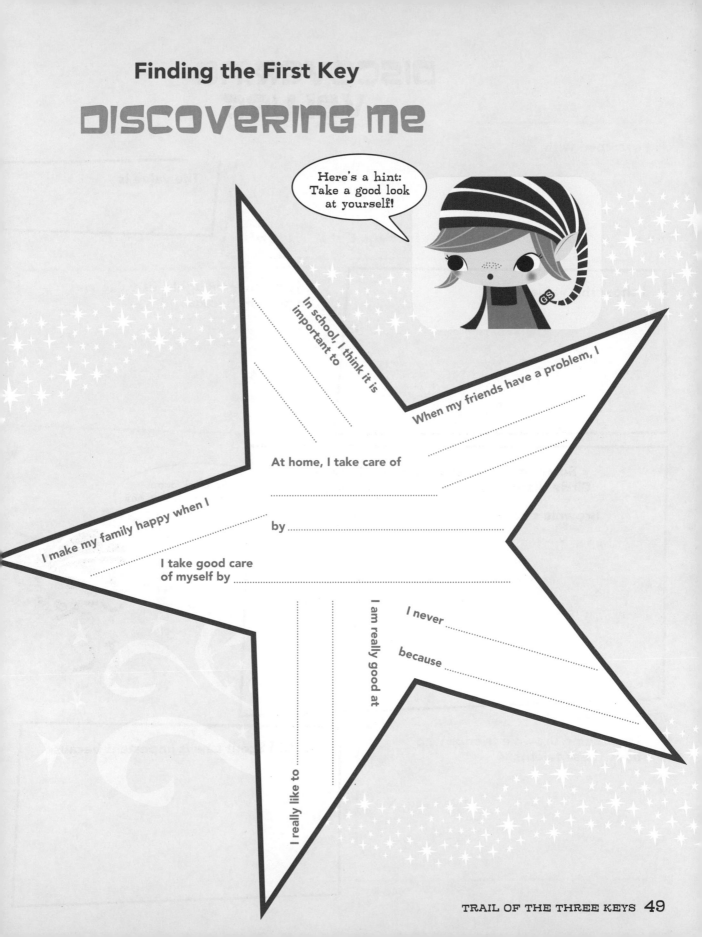

Here's a hint: Take a good look at yourself!

In school, I think it is important to

When my friends have a problem, I

At home, I take care of

I make my family happy when I

by

I take good care of myself by

I am really good at

I never

because

I really like to

DISCOVERING VALUES

I searched with

and discovered a value from the Girl Scout Law!

The value is

I show this value by

My partner thought this value was important because

Some of the other girls in our Brownie Circle discovered these talents and values:

Brownie's name	Values

These Girl Scout Brownies sure know how to see their values!

I met some Brownie friends who have these talents:

The Girl Scout Law is important because

DISCOVERING FAMILY

I read the Girl Scout Law with my family.
Then I asked them to tell me one value
of the Law that they think is really, really
important in our family.

We show we care about this value when we

The value is

Some other talents I am proud
to see in my family are:

Talents

Names

My family thinks it is important because

Yoo-hoo, Brownie
Elf, where's our family
star? And where are *you*?
Oh — I sent you
on a quest!

The First Key

I Found My .... Key

As a Girl Scout Brownie, I discovered that I can use my skills and values in the world around me. I found the key because I realized:

1. A special skill I have is ....

2. A value from the Girl Scout Law that is important to me is ....

....

3. A value from the Girl Scout Law my family cares about is ....

....

We show it by ....

....

Signed   **Date**

What did you and your Brownie friends say when you found the first key?

....

....

What does it look like when you and your Brownie friends go ELF? Draw it!

Searching for the Second Key

MAKING A BROWNIE TEAM AGREEMENT

In our Brownie group, we meet at

....

We promise to act like a team —
to listen
and to help each other.
We all think these things are important.

And our team thinks it's important to ....

....

....

....

....

....

In "The ELF Adventure," Campbell, Alejandra, and Jamila agreed to meet at the park and plan what they could do to save the trees.

Here's a hint: Take a good look around you!

BICYCLES, BALLS, & SPORTS STUFF

REAL UNHEALTHY KIDS MEAL

FAKE CANNED FOOD · Chemical Puffs · Salty Dogs

ALL SUGAR COOKIES · salty salt potato bites · SUGARY STIX

SUGAR PLUS COLA · no vitamins SPRITZ

SUPER DUPER SUGAR FIZZ

What's Happening at Campbell's House?

Along the Trail of the Three Keys, Brownies care about their friends — and their families. Take a look at Campbell's house. What can she do to show she cares about her family?

Campbell Cares

Give Campbell some ideas for leading her family to feeling better:

Little sister Sage needs less .... **and more** ....

Unpack the .... **and go outside to** ....

Mom can have some fun with us if she puts the .... **on the dog and takes us all out for a** .... **to the** ....

Go shopping and get some .... **and** .... **to make a yummy and healthy snack!**

Do you remember Campbell's new dog's name?

Hint: You may need to get back on the Trail of the Elf Adventure.

It's Your Turn

Show your family you care by leading them to try a new healthy habit. Choose what you will ask your family to do with you:

✓ **Go for a walk or bike ride together, maybe at the** ....

✓ **Make a healthy snack to enjoy together, like** ....

✓ **Drink more water and less** ....

✓ **Play an active game like** .... **to get us all moving.**

✓ ....

....

(something you think of yourself!)

Some "What-ifs"

Suppose you can't get anybody to walk with you? They say, "Too tired" or "Too much to do."

• **Do what Campbell did. She and her mom took Sage on a walk and played a little game along the way — they made a list of all the animals they saw (birds, squirrels, even bugs) and gave them the craziest names they could think up.**

• **Make your time together as fun as you like.**

DO YOU AND YOUR FAMILY LIKE TO EAT SWEETS?

Then try a recipe like this one:

BAKED APPLES

You will need:
- 1 baking apple for each person
- ¼ cup unsweetened apple juice for each apple
- 2 tablespoons of raisins for each apple
- 1 marshmallow for each apple
- 1 teaspoon ground cinnamon

1. Have an adult help you peel the apple halfway down. Core the apple almost to its bottom.

2. Stuff the apple core with raisins.

3. Put the apple in a baking dish and pour the juice over it.

4. Sprinkle the apple with a little cinnamon.

5. Bake the apple in an oven at 375° F for 40-45 minutes. Then put a marshmallow on top of each apple and let it melt.

Check that the apple is tender, but not mushy.

Enjoy this treat hot or cold!

More Brownie Team Recipes
Try these with your family — or Brownie friends.

FRUIT JUICE FIZZ

You will need:
- 1 orange or lemon
- Orange juice
- Pineapple juice
- Cranberry juice
- Seltzer or club soda

1. Cut the orange or lemon into slices.

2. Put 1 or 2 cups of each juice into a pitcher.

3. For every 3 cups of juice, add 1 cup of seltzer. (If you have a total of 6 cups of juice, you will need 2 cups of seltzer.)

4. Add the slices of fruit.

5. Refrigerate until the juice is chilled.

6. Serve.

Write a recipe for a healthy and good drink you like:

....

....

....

....

....

Remember fruits and veggies every day! What did you eat today that was green (and not candy!)?

SURPRISING FRUIT DIPS

You will need:
- 1 package semisweet chocolate chips
- ½ cup skim milk
- 3 apples
- 3 pears
- Wax paper, placed over a cookie sheet or large plate

1. With help from an adult, core apples and pears and cut them into thin slices.

2. Put chocolate pieces and ¼ cup of the milk in a microwave-safe bowl or measuring cup.

3. Heat for 30 seconds on high.

4. Stir.

5. Then heat again until all the chocolate pieces have completely melted.

6. Add more milk gradually and stir until the sauce is smooth but not thin.

7. Dip the fruit into the chocolate, place on wax paper, and chill for 15 minutes or until the chocolate is firm.

You can use other fruits, too, such as bananas, oranges, strawberries, and kiwis.

DYNAMITE DIP

Carrots, cucumbers, jicama, celery, peppers, and broccoli go with Dynamite Dip.

You will need:
- One 16-ounce carton of low-fat or nonfat plain yogurt
- One 3-ounce package of low-fat or nonfat cream cheese
- ½ cup light or nonfat ranch dressing
- 2 tablespoons parsley flakes or dill, or chopped fresh parsley or dill

Put the yogurt, cream cheese, ranch dressing, and parsley or dill in a bowl. Stir them all together with a big spoon.

CARING ABOUT YOUR FAMILY

Brownie's name

I showed my family I care about their health!
I led my family to be healthier by

This is how we had fun:

This is what we learned:

Signed   **Date**

make a Family Fun Jar

With members of your family, make suggestions for active family fun. Put the suggestions in a decorated jar, and pull them out for a get-active boost. Some ideas:

- **Ride bikes.**
- **Walk around the neighborhood looking for something new: a fountain, a garden, a new store, a neighbor's garden with new flowers.**
- **When watching TV, take a jumping-jacks break every time a commercial comes on.**
- **Have a crazy relay race: Find something silly you have to carry or pass as you run.**

WHAT COLOR IS YOUR FOOD?

What's in your food rainbow? Only white bread and white potatoes? Add some color to your plate —

- **pink salmon or tuna**
- **dark green spinach or peas**
- **a mixed salad of light green lettuce, red peppers, and orange carrots**

Keep a color food diary for two days.

MY FOOD DIARY

Today I ate these foods: ....

....

Their colors were: ....

....

These colors were missing from my day: ....

....

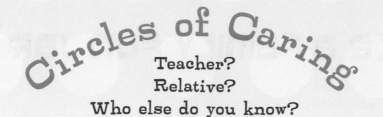

Circles of Caring

Teacher?
Relative?
Who else do you know?

Brownies make connections with other people. Imagine:
You're in the center
of all who matter most to you.
Think about all the circles around you
and put in the names of people you know and love.

BROWNIES CARE ABOUT THEIR COMMUNITIES

Green Falls
Public Library

Green Falls Apts

STOP

Look at this trash!

Where are we going to ride our bikes?

Why don't you two come out to my family's *rancho*!

IMPROVING LIFE IN GREEN FALLS
What's wrong with this picture? Circle anything you think needs fixing or improving.

The blank lines are for your ideas to make Green Falls a friendly place — for everybody.

....

....

....

WHAT COULD MAKE THIS

What do you think people could do to help?

Hector and his mother are deaf, but his sister and father can hear. Hector wants to be just like other kids and ride his bike and play ball outside. **Hector could play outside if**

....

....

....

Nana Gina is a grandmother. She can walk well, but she can't drive anymore. She likes to live close to a doctor's office and a supermarket. **Nana Gina needs a neighbor to**

....

....

....

Marsha uses a wheelchair to get around her house and neighborhood. She always looks happy and likes to be as active as she can. **Marsha might like a visitor because**

....

....

....

Shawn lost his sight when he was a baby. He is 16 now. He has a seeing-eye dog named Charlie. He lives with his mom and aunt. **When Shawn wants to go to a new place, he needs**

....

....

....

NEIGHBORHOOD BETTER?

What can a community offer to make each person's life easier and safer? For example, what could a community have so that Shawn can walk about his neighborhood safely?

THINK AND TALK ABOUT...

Some answers —
- Smooth sidewalks
- Beeping stop signals that he can hear at every corner
- Braille on signs so he can read them

Who else might benefit from these things?

Does your community have these things?

How could Gina get to the supermarket?

What would happen if Marsha needed to get into a building that had steps in front?

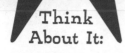

CARING ABOUT YOUR COMMUNITY

Think About It:

- **Who did these kids worry about?**

- **Why did the kids decide to write a letter?**

- **What happened after they wrote the letter?**

- **If you wanted to fix something in your community, what would it be?**

- **What would you write in your letter?**

The Case of the Broken Sidewalk

Miss Jeanne's preschool class loved to visit the park near their school. One day, as they left the park, Lucy tripped on a rough spot in the sidewalk and fell. She scraped both her knees.

Miss Jeanne cleaned and bandaged Lucy's knees, and all the class gathered around her. "The sidewalk's all broken," Peter said. "That's why Lucy fell. We've got to fix this sidewalk so kids don't get hurt!"

Lucy felt a little better. "Once I watched a sidewalk getting made. There was a cement truck, and workers were using tools to make the sidewalk smooth," she said.

Miss Jeanne said, "Taking care of the sidewalks is the job of city workers, like the people you saw, Lucy." Then she asked the children, "How do you think we could get their help with this sidewalk?"

"We could show them the broken sidewalk," said Peter.

"Lucy, you better show them your hurt knees," said Sara.

"I know! Let's write them a letter!" said Megan.

Miss Jeanne wrote down all the children's ideas. When they got back to class, she asked them to vote on what they wanted to do. Together they decided to write a letter to the mayor. In the letter, they would tell her about the problem with the sidewalk.

One day, the class got a letter back. The mayor's letter thanked the children for being concerned about the sidewalk. The mayor also wrote that she would take note of their suggestions for fixing it. Miss Jeanne's students were so happy and proud.

I Found My _____ Key

As a Girl Scout Brownie, I shared my skills and talents with others around me.

To find the key, I figured out that ....
....
....

I show my family I care when I ....
....
....

I care about my community by ....
....
....

....

Signed   **Date**

When you found the second key, what did you and your Brownie friends say?

....

Have you lost your way? Check your map. Fill in the steps you've just taken to get where you are!

THE BROWNIE BRAINSTORM

On the Trail of the ELF Adventure, the Brownie friends save a tree family. What is your Brownie Team going to do for your community?

What places might need the Brownie Team?

Here's a hint: How can you make the world a better place?

What could we do? Here's what we look like in action!

Two Brownie Songs

Now that you've decided what you will do for your community, how about cheering yourself on with some songs?

Brownie Hiking Song

We are the happy Brownies.
We are the busy elves.
We love to help each other.
And, of course, we help ourselves.
We wake up in the morning
    with a smile upon each face.
And even if things don't go right
We keep that smile in place.
We're the happy Brownies!

Brownie Smile Song

I've something in my pocket.
It belongs across my face.
And I keep it very close at hand
In a most convenient place.

I'm sure you couldn't guess it
If you guessed a long, long while.
So I'll take it out and put it on —
It's a great big Brownie Smile!

THINK and FLY INTO
BROWNIES
acTion

What do you think about what you have been doing?

1. Our Brownie Team is taking action to

2. We met and learned a lot about our project from

3. We have a plan, and our goal is

4. The job I like best is

(figuring out a budget? asking people for help? setting up and organizing? making a poster? other things?)

5. The biggest need we want to meet is

6. It feels really good when

The Brownie Team

"FLYING INTO ACTION" CHECKLIST

Which items did your team do to complete the three steps to find the third key?

* We found **places** where we think we can be useful.

* We thought about **who** might need us and what we could do.

* We made a **team decision**.

* We made some of the **preparations** for the action we were taking.

* We're beginning to **understand** how our efforts will make a difference.

* We met some of the **people** from the place we chose for action, and we hope to keep in touch with them.

* We **took action** — and this is what we did ....

  ....

* We **reflected** on the project and added our ideas to our Making Memories pages in our Quest books.

* We celebrated and **earned** our third key.

The Third Key

I Found My .... Key

My Brownie Team identified a place in our community where we could ....

....

We created a plan to ....

We made the world better by ....

....

....

....

Signed .... **Date**

What do you and your Brownie friends say about the third key?

....

....

....

....

....

Check the special Girl Scout leadership qualities
you feel you have gained:

☆ I have lots of talents.

☆ I feel confident in all that I have contributed to
this Quest.

☆ I can lead my family.

☆ I have fun with other Girl Scout Brownies.

☆ I feel powerful by doing my Take Action Project.

Keep it GOING

Wow, that's a pretty special lock! It needs all three keys to open. And you have them all! Congratulations!

Now I know what I can do with my three keys!

When I use all three, I'm a ....

A .... is a person who .... and

.... and ....

The keys are yours!
They will open many doors
to more exciting adventures
as a ....
in Girl Scouts — and in life!

JULIETTE GORDON LOW AND THE THREE KEYS

Juliette Gordon Low's nickname was "Daisy." Here are some highlights from her life.

When the United States entered World War I, Daisy asked Girl Scouts to volunteer in hospitals, sew for the Red Cross, assist servicemen at railroad stations, and grow vegetables.

In 1917, she organized the first troop in the United States for girls with physical disabilities.

Daisy started the first Girl Scout troop with 18 girls in Savannah, Georgia, on March 12, 1912.

Daisy paid all the expenses to keep the Girl Scouts going; when the money ran out, she sold her pearls.

Daisy made her plans and acted upon them. She often said, "Whatever you take up, do it with all your might and stick to it!"

Daisy believed in wasting nothing. She really did live the Girl Scout Law!

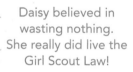

When there was a disagreement, Daisy would say, "Let's ask the girls. They will decide whether the plan is good or not. You can trust them to know."

Juliette Gordon Low, 1887, by Edward Hughes (1832-1908). Oil on canvas. The National Portrait Gallery, Smithsonian Institution, Washington, D.C.

Most of all, Daisy loved spending time with the girls. She often said to other volunteers, "We must never lose sight of the girls. The girls must come first."

She loved to dance. Even her camping house had a place for girls to dance and have tea.

DAISY LOW KNEW
WHAT IT TAKES TO BE A _____

DAISY AND THE FIRST KEY

What were Daisy's special qualities and values?

Hint: You'll find the answers in the highlights of her life.

DAISY AND THE SECOND KEY

How did Daisy team up with girls?

DAISY AND THE THIRD KEY

How did Daisy make the world a better place?

If Daisy were here today, I'd want to talk to her about

I would like to thank Daisy for

Daisy would be happy because our Brownie Team

Making Memories

What are three keys you can't use to open doors?

TURKEY

MONKEY

DONKEY

I have changed
my troop by a lot.
Now they have
more confidence
in themselves, and
that has helped a
lot in our journey.
— Samantha, 9,
California

Making Memories

Girl Scouts
has made me
put others before
myself. I always
have fun at
Girl Scouts!
— Gaby, 9,
Missouri

I LOVE BEING A GIRL SCOUT! Girl Scouting helps me respect my family, people around me, and the environment.
— Emily, 9, Ohio

Making Memories

Girl Scouts
helps me keep
my mind on real
important things.
— Tatianna, 10,
Pennsylvania

I feel that if my
troop works hard, we
can change the world.
— Mika, 9, Texas

Making Memories